Editors' Preface to Macmillan Studi

The rapid growth of academic lit
ics has posed serious problems f
of the subject. The latter find it difficult to keep pace with more
than a few areas of their subject, so that an inevitable trend
towards specialism emerges. The student quickly loses perspec-
tive as the maze of theories and models grows and the discipline
accommodates an increasing amount of quantitative techniques.

'Macmillan Studies in Economics' is a new series which sets
out to provide the student with short, reasonably critical sur-
veys of the developments within the various specialist areas of
theoretical and applied economics. At the same time, the studies
aim to form an integrated series so that, seen as a whole, they
supply a balanced overview of the subject of economics. The
emphasis in each study is upon recent work, but each topic will
generally be placed in a historical context so that the reader may
see the logical development of thought through time. Selected
bibliographies are provided to guide readers to more extensive
works. Each study aims at a brief treatment of the salient problems in order to avoid clouding the issues in detailed argument.
Nonetheless, the texts are largely self-contained, and presume
only that the student has some knowledge of elementary micro-
economics and macro-economics.

Mathematical exposition has been adopted only where
necessary. Some recent developments in economics are not
readily comprehensible without some mathematics and statistics, and quantitative approaches also serve to shorten what
would otherwise be lengthy and involved arguments. Where
authors have found it necessary to introduce mathematical
techniques, these techniques have been kept to a minimum.
The emphasis is upon the economics, and not upon the quantitative methods. Later studies in the series will provide analyses
of the links between quantitative methods, in particular econo-
metrics, and economic analysis.

MACMILLAN STUDIES IN ECONOMICS

General Editors: D. C. ROWAN and G. R. FISHER

Executive Editor: D. W. PEARCE

Published

John Burton: WAGE INFLATION
Miles Fleming: MONETARY THEORY
C. J. Hawkins and D. W. Pearce: CAPITAL INVESTMENT APPRAISAL
David F. Heathfield: PRODUCTION FUNCTIONS
J. E. King: LABOUR ECONOMICS
D. W. Pearce: COST-BENEFIT ANALYSIS
Maurice Peston: PUBLIC GOODS AND THE PUBLIC SECTOR
David Robertson: INTERNATIONAL TRADE POLICY
G. K. Shaw: FISCAL POLICY
R. Shone: THE PURE THEORY OF INTERNATIONAL TRADE
Frank J. B. Stilwell: REGIONAL ECONOMIC POLICY
Grahame Walshe: INTERNATIONAL MONETARY REFORM

Forthcoming

E. R. Chang: PRINCIPLES OF ECONOMIC ACCOUNTING
G. Denton: ECONOMICS OF INDICATIVE PLANNING
N. Gibson: MONETARY POLICY
C. J. Hawkins: THEORY OF THE FIRM
Dudley Jackson: ACCOUNTING FOR POVERTY
P. N. Junankar: INVESTMENT FUNCTIONS
J. A. Kregel: THE THEORY OF ECONOMIC GROWTH
D. Mayston: THE POSSIBILITY OF SOCIAL CHOICE
G. McKenzie: MONETARY THEORY OF INTERNATIONAL TRADE
S. K. Nath: WELFARE ECONOMICS
A. Peaker: BRITISH ECONOMIC GROWTH SINCE 1945
F. Pennance: HOUSING ECONOMICS
Charles K. Rowley: ANTI-TRUST ECONOMICS
C. Sharp: TRANSPORT ECONOMICS
P. Simmons: DEMAND THEORY
M. Stabler: AGRICULTURAL ECONOMICS
John Vaizey: ECONOMICS OF EDUCATION
P. Victor: ECONOMICS OF POLLUTION
J. Wiseman: PRICING PROBLEMS OF THE NATIONALISED INDUSTRIES

Public Goods and the Public Sector

MAURICE PESTON

Professor of Economics, Queen Mary College, University of London

Macmillan

First published 1972 by
THE MACMILLAN PRESS LTD
London and Basingstoke
Associated companies in New York Toronto
Dublin Melbourne Johannesburg and Madras

SBN 333 12403 0

Printed in Great Britain by
THE ANCHOR PRESS LTD
Tiptree, Essex

Contents

Acknowledgements

I am indebted to the editors of the series and to Hugh Gravelle for valuable comments on the first draft. They are, of course, not responsible for the final content, with which I know Mr Gravelle is in some disagreement.

M. P.

1 Taxonomy

The economist's interest in public goods arises from his interest in the public sector and is concerned in large part with offering a positive explanation to account for what governments do and a normative justification for what they ought to do. Goods and services are not provided simply by households and firms, but also by government. In addition, apart from engaging directly in the provision of goods and services, the public sector acts to regulate and control, to tax and subsidise the private sector. Now, while it may be that some of this activity is arbitrary or, at least, is not explicable within the framework of economics, there is a considerable body of economic theory which can throw some light on it, and which it is the purpose of this survey to explore. In particular, we shall try and convey to the reader some of the fundamental ideas that have emerged in recent controversies which not only clarify the role of the public sector but are also beginning to lead to a reconsideration of the theory of the private sector too. Much of the work that has been published is extremely difficult and will certainly continue to be studied and reinterpreted for many years yet. The introductory and tentative nature of what follows cannot, therefore, be emphasised too strongly. In addition, there is no substitute for the serious reader for reading the items in the Select Bibliography and the great quantity of further material discussed in the quoted articles and books.

In elementary economics we assume that the goods and services that people use are of concern only to themselves. We analyse the economic system in terms of two sorts of decision units, firms and households, each of them basing its decisions on the goods and services it buys and sells. The firm may purchase factors of production which it uses to produce products to sell for a profit. The household sells factors of production and uses its income to purchase products. In each case the behaviour of any decision unit is of no direct concern to any other decision unit. In more formal terms, the variables in the firm's revenue function are the goods it sells, and in its production function the factors it buys. The variables in the household's utility function are the goods it consumes, and in its budget constraint the goods it buys and the factors it sells.

This does not mean that the decision units are entirely independent of each other. The factors of production that the firm buys are the factors of production that the household sells; the goods that the firm sells are the goods that the household buys.[1] An increase in the demand for a commodity produced under conditions of diminishing returns will make the existing purchasers of it worse off. Altogether, we usually go to great pains to emphasise the interdependent nature of the decision units comprising an economic system.

There is, however, a second kind of interdependence in the economic system which requires analysis. Certain commodities that people buy may actually enter directly into the utility functions, or cost functions, or production functions of others. Certain activities engaged in by one decision unit may have a direct impact on the economic situation of other decision units. The phenomena we have in mind are called external economies and diseconomies,[2] and akin to them are what are called

[1] Firms also trade with each other, of course. Equally, unless we define our units so as to make it impossible, households trade with each other.

[2] They are also sometimes called neighbourhood effects or spillovers, or external effects, or social effects, or social costs and benefits. Instead of public goods we also sometimes refer to collective goods. We shall take the broad view and use all equivalent expressions interchangeably.

It is worth noting, however, that in practice public goods are usually discussed in terms of desirable phenomena. In fact, this is not a necessary characteristic of what we want to examine. We can think of public goods as being beneficial or harmful depending on the particular case, or we can invent an expression *public bads* to deal with the undesirable phenomena. My own preference is for the former, but there is no real objection to the latter formulation. Similarly, while external economies are beneficial and external diseconomies harmful, the other equivalent expressions do not distinguish the cases. For them we may refer to beneficial or harmful neighbourhood effects, beneficial or harmful spillovers, etc.

public goods. Alternatively, we may stress the word 'public' and treat external economies and diseconomies as activities with a public-good content, the extreme case of which is the pure public good.

Again, to make a formal statement: in the case of a household a *potential externality* exists if its utility function or constraints contain variables which are under the control of or belong to other households or firms; in the case of the firm a *potential externality* exists if its production function or objective function contain variables which are under the control of or belong to other households or firms. We use the expression 'potential externality' because this kind of direct interdependence can exist without affecting the behaviour or certain of the optimality conditions of welfare economics.[1]

Although the distinction between criterion functions and constraints is not clear-cut, and is frequently simply a matter of how a particular problem is formulated, most writers have tended to emphasise externalities as appearing in the utility function of the household or the production function of the firm. Of course, once the firm is assumed to have a more general objective than profit maximising, it too will have a utility function, and it will be natural to consider externalities as arising there. Equally, however, in the case of the household it may be appropriate to analyse certain problems in terms of externalities affecting its choice set rather than its preferences. If, for

[1] Buchanan and Stubblebine [8] define an externality in much the same way as we define a potential externality, except that they emphasise the utility function rather than the constraints. They were, however, the first to make clear that the externality may have no effect at the margin, and may be irrelevant to behaviour. One way of making this clearer still is to use the word 'potential' in the definition. The connection between public goods and externalities is rather complicated, and we shall not deal with it fully here. The matter is raised in an extremely interesting way in Mishan [25], following on some remarks of Margolis [19]. One difficulty is that public goods are frequently defined in purely technical or institutional terms, while externalities are defined in terms of such economic concepts as utility functions and production functions. A second difficulty is related to the need to distinguish the physical quantity of the good from the number of people consuming it, total consumption being the product of the two (see Millward [23]). My own view is that externality is the fundamental concept.

11

example, it is allocating scarce time as well as scarce income, congestion will represent an external effect in its time constraint. Similarly, all the usual gardening externalities connected with weeding, drainage, fences, shade-producing trees, etc., may be analysed according to their influence on the set of available alternatives.

The kind of general interdependence we have defined in our opening discussion can now be examined a little more closely.

As far as public goods are concerned, the following points are usually made:

(a) The provision of any quantity of the good to an individual implies the provision of the same quantity to a group of individuals.

(b) In the provision of the good it is not possible to restrict its consumption to particular individuals.

(c) In the provision of the good it is not optimal to restrict its consumption to particular individuals.

(d) Related to (b), a public good is one which it is impossible to charge for.

(e) Related to (c), a public good is one which it is not optimal to charge for.

(f) Given that the good is provided for one or several people, it can be freely or virtually freely provided for others as well.

Some economists then go on to restrict the definition of public goods to one of these categories. Since, however, all these characteristics of goods are interesting, we shall not rule out any of them from our discussions at this stage. Instead, we shall consider the following taxonomy:

(i) The good if provided to one is provided to all. Call this *non-excludability* and its opposite *excludability*.

(ii) The consumption to the full of a particular quantity of the good by one person does not impede the consumption of that same quantity by others. Call this *non-rivalness* and its opposite *rivalness* (see Head [17]).

Goods then fall into four categories as in the following tableau:

	Excludable	*Non-excludable*
Rival	A	B
Non-rival	C	D

A. RIVAL AND EXCLUDABLE GOODS

Here we have the case of what might be called the normal private good. This is provided to the individual person, and the fact that he consumes it means that nobody else can consume it. (In the case of a durable good we refer, of course, to its consumption at a point of time, but it is worth noting that a durable private good providing services through time has some of the quality of non-rivalness in that its use by one person at one time does not preclude its use by another person later. Of course, the services of the good at different points of time may not be perfect substitutes, and user costs may also arise, so that some degree of rivalness may usually be involved.)

B. RIVAL NON-EXCLUDABLE GOODS

Here we have a good, one person's consumption of which rules out others', but where the provider is unable to decide who is to be the consumer. The sort of example that economists delight in is the case of bees which fertilise flowers, but the bee-keeper is unable to select which flower-grower is to receive this benefit. Similarly, a flower-grower is unable to select which bees receive his honey. There may be partial selection via location, but any additional bee-keeper or flower-grower can enter the district. Thus, the flowers are rival, but no flower can be excluded from a particular bee, and the bees are rival, but no bee can be excluded from a particular flower. A generalisation of this case would be that of quasi-rivalness, namely, where consumption of the good by one person lowers the benefits of its consumption to others rather than reducing it to zero. An example would be free access to roads or pavements which then became congested.[1]

[1] Not all economists would accept these generalisations to the main example of B or the returns to scale extension of C.

Another extension of this case would be where exclusion was unacceptable for institutional reasons or was prohibitively expensive. The occupation of a particular place on a beach or a road would be a suitable example.

C. NON-RIVAL EXCLUDABLE GOODS

In this case it is possible to prevent individual people enjoying the relevant benefit, but the fact that anyone is so prevented does not actually allow anybody else the benefit. Exclusion may be physically possible even though one person's consumption does not preclude others'. The obvious example is a theatre performance where the demand is less than capacity even when admission is not charged. Another example would be an uncongested bridge or road.

What we are saying in this case is that the marginal cost of an additional person's consumption is zero, but not that the marginal cost of an additional physical quantity is zero.

A possible extension of this case would be where exclusion is possible, but the provision of the good to some means that it can be provided very cheaply to others. Some examples of increasing returns to scale with marginal cost much less than average cost would come under this heading, especially if the overhead costs had already been met by some consumers.

D. NON-RIVAL AND NON-EXCLUDABLE GOODS

This is the case usually referred to as the pure public good. If it is provided for some it is available to all and it is impossible to prevent anybody from enjoying it. The obvious example is national defence. Its provision for any individual implies its provision for all the other citizens of the nation, and the fact that any one person is defended does not restrict the extent to which any other person is defended.

A further point to mention here is that the same 'good' may fall into one category in one set of circumstances and into another category in other sets. For this reason, although this taxonomy is extremely useful, it is not the whole story, and the classification of particular activities in practice is by no means obvious.[1]

Having produced this taxonomy and cited examples of goods which confer benefits on people, it is worth while seeing if we can find other corresponding examples in terms of bads. Case A will obviously consist of any commodity which an individual person dislikes. He will avoid the consumption of that commodity unless it is necessary to the consumption of some other commodity which he does like. In that case it would be the cost or part of the cost of the beneficial commodity.

Case B is more complicated because we have to be clear as to what 'non-excludable' is taken to mean. What is required is that the provider of the public bad cannot discriminate between those who suffer and those who do not. An example would be the bees again. Their owner cannot exclude anybody from the chance of being stung, but one person stung by a particular bee will prevent someone else being stung by the same bee. Similarly, a killer driver may not be able to select whom he kills on the motorway, but in killing one and himself he saves temporarily all the others.

Case C is also a trifle complicated. What we are looking for is a circumstance where it is possible for the source to discriminate between the individual recipients, yet where one person's consumption does not limit another person's. One possible example would be a contagious disease where the carrier can choose whom he comes into contact with. Another would be cigarette smoking, which may be on such a scale that whole theatres or restaurants may be polluted and the harm is non-rival. Nonetheless, smoking areas may be set aside at zero or low cost, making exclusion possible. Exclusion may even be a simple matter of organisation, e.g. smoking upstairs in buses or in special compartments in trains.

Case D would be the direct counterpart to a public good and would be, therefore, a pure public bad. Just as national security was earlier cited as a public good, poor defence and foreign policies generating national insecurity would be public bads. In placing any citizen in jeopardy, all citizens are placed in jeopardy. Virtually all examples of large-scale environmental pollution are public bads in that nobody can be excluded and the damage to one does not limit the damage to others. To revert to the costs of exclusion, the cigarette smoke example may

[1] I am indebted to Hugh Gravelle for this point.

15

become case D if these are high, as is alleged to be the case in some aircraft.[1] This leads to the obvious point that, depending on differences of opinion concerning the effects of particular actions or their desirability, the same thing may be regarded as a public good by some, a public bad by others, and be viewed indifferently by a third group. In the extreme case the public good generated by military activity in one nation may be a public bad to another, enemy nation. To revert to our example of the bees, the spraying of crops by farmers may kill large numbers of bees. This will be a public bad, case D, if the spraying is large relative to the number of bees, or non-excludable rivalness, case B, if there is limited spraying. Again, this is partly a matter of interpretation. More spray for one bee means less for another. If we think in terms of 'spraying', however, one bee's liability to be sprayed may not affect another's. Incidentally, the harm of the spraying will be felt by the bee-keepers and the flower-growers. It will also be seen as a benefit by people who would otherwise be stung. This illustrates the point that the normal interdependence of the economic system also applies to public goods, and that those immediately affected need not be the same as those ultimately affected.

Let us now examine the phenomenon of excludability a little more closely. We have explained already that we are considering exclusion from the point of view of the provider (or operator or direct user) of the good or service. If the activity is harmful to any other individual, he may still be able to exclude himself from it by taking appropriate counteraction.[2] The bee-keeper

[1] Important articles on pollution are Bohm [5] and Mishan [25].

[2] This is one of the many significant points that emerge from the seminal article by Coase [11]. What had been a rather moribund part of economics has in the past decade come alive and extremely exciting intellectually because of this article and its subsequent development by J. M. Buchanan. It is rather curious that the theory of public goods and externalities, which is an important strand in the justification of public-sector activity, should in recent years have been most advanced by a group of economists who have a predilection for anti-interventionism and the market-place. In fact their critique of the earlier theory, while demolishing the case for naïve interventionism itself, gives rise to a much more powerful case. Certainly, there would be no reduction of interventionism if governments were encouraged to deal with all cases of externality, let alone other examples of market failure.

16

may not be able to determine which people his bees sting, but an individual may be able to wear protective clothing or cover himself in bee repellent, or even move away from where the bees are. Equally, the broadcasting service may not be able to exclude anyone from listening in, but a prerequisite of listening will be the purchase of, or at least access to, a wireless set. Incidentally, the large-scale purchase of wireless and mono-chrome TV receivers indicates a desire for private viewing of or listening to a public service, although public viewing or listening might be cheaper depending on the value of an individual person's time. Colour TV sets, however, at the moment in the U.K., are viewed to a considerable extent in public places, and up to the capacity of a bar in a public house are more akin to public goods. This suggests that the range of possibilities for individual exclusion may be fairly large.[1] Equally, the number of examples where the provider of the service may be able to practise exclusion, but at a cost, may be larger than is sometimes imagined. If we take law and order, which is usually viewed as a public good under case D, it is apparent that in principle the services of the constabulary could be made available only to those who had subscribed to them. This might for general purposes be inefficient and costly, but it is feasible. Of course, if the criminal is uncertain as to who will be defended, a measure of protection will be offered to non-subscribers, especially if the number of criminals declines as the rate of return to criminal activity is reduced. This means that there may be a public-good content to this activity which is a residual element of non-excludability. Similarly, a fire service can, in principle, be provided on an exclusive basis, but even there some of its benefits may spill over as public goods to non-subscribers.

Of course, the costs of exclusion may be so high that if the service is to be provided on that basis, or not at all, it will not, in fact, be provided. It could be, for example, that the costs of a system of ticket collection in a railway service are so high that

[1] Note that the feasibility of exclusion does not imply its opti-mality. Note also that rivalness may be a definitional matter. The occupation of a particular seat in a theatre by one person prevents its occupation by another. But the relevant variable may not be seats but the ability to watch, which will be non-rival at less than full capacity.

for no desired quantity of the service can the price charged to individuals cover total costs. Despite this, it is possible that the value people place on particular quantities of the service could be above its average costs (other than of the charging system itself), and therefore that the provision of the service apart from the ticket collection is prima facie desirable.[1]

Another aspect of exclusion which will be dealt with below is that it may be feasible and cheap, and yet suboptimal. Thus, exclusion is concerned directly with the possibility of the market provision of the good. What is optimal depends on the alternatives available. It may be perfectly possible to charge individuals for the use of a service. What is more, a charging policy may exist which would enable a private organisation to make a profit. Nonetheless, it could still happen that it would be better to provide the service at no charge on a non-excludable basis. The obvious example is the theatre operating at less than full capacity. Equally, of course, in other cases exclusion may be possible, though expensive, and the free market may be optimal.

Before venturing further into theory, it may be helpful now to mention the various sorts of activities that are considered to fall into this field, bearing in mind that not all of them are pure public goods, and some have only a minimal public-good content. Firstly, one has in mind the provision of law and order and defence (i.e. internal and external security). Connected with this are such diverse functions as the enforcement of contracts, the arbitration of private conflict, military conscription, the drawing up and enforcement of driving regulations. Secondly, there are regulations concerning public health and education and the public finance and provision of these things. Thirdly, there are a great variety of town-planning and building regulations. Fourthly, there is concern with traffic congestion. Fifthly, there are the problems of noise, of pollution of the environment, preservation of the countryside, old buildings, etc. Sixthly, there is public provision and subsidy of the arts (visual, performing, and so on), the formation of taste, education, etc. Lastly, but possibly encompassing all the rest, is public concern with the preservation of society and the interests of future generations.

Of all these it has been said: 'These are the public goods. Law

[1] This somewhat paradoxical case will be discussed further below, p. 54.

and order is an example, and there are many others too familiar to make further exemplification worth while.'[1] Another distinguished economist has asserted: 'I believe . . . that some of the most pressing economic problems of our time do call for government action and call for it on grounds which are essentially based on an extension of the externalities argument.'[2]

Two other quotations from leading economists may cause us not to become too optimistic about theory and practice in this area. Paul Samuelson [37] has written: 'My doubts do not assert that passably good organisation of the public household is impossible or unlikely, but merely that theorists have not yet provided us with much analysis of these matters that has validity or plausibility.' Twelve years earlier Graaf [16] stated: 'A theory which takes external effects in consumption into account seems to become so hopelessly complicated that any chance of ever applying it becomes exceedingly remote.'[3]

There is one other economist who must be quoted here simply to emphasise further the point that there is a fair gap between the theory of public goods and its actual application, and also

[1] Dorfman [12]. I do not agree with Dorfman that exemplification is not worth while. As a matter of fact it is not obvious what is the set of public goods, and one objective of political activity is to agree as to its contents.

[2] Baumol [4]. The introduction to this book is the best available survey of the literature up to 1965, although it seems to do less than justice to the originality of Coase's contribution. It does, however, make clear what was not clear in the first edition, namely, that 'the presence of externalities does *not* automatically justify government intervention'. Clearly, every busybody is asserting the existence of widespread external diseconomies but this is not even prima facie evidence of the failure of the market and the need for governmental activity.

Although I do not disagree with Baumol, it is important not to ignore other economic problems as well which, while they can be fitted into the externalities framework, tend to get ignored in the context of present-day emphasis on environment. My personal view is that inequities in lifetime income, consumption distribution and work experience still remain the dominant problem for public action in the U.S. and the U.K.

[3] Of course, it may be possible that public intervention based on externalities raises welfare even though all the niceties of the economic analysis are not taken into account.

that one man's benefit is another man's cost. Milton Friedman [15] says: 'we shall always want to enter on the liability side of any proposed government intervention its neighbourhood effect on threatening freedom, and give this considerable weight.'[1]

[1] While not denying that government activity also has neighbour-hood effects, and that a particular form of these is to fail to compensate individuals correctly, it seems strange to inhabitants of the U.K. to see such undue concentration on the state as an enemy of freedom. For most people the danger seems remote, especially compared with the activities of the private sector here and in the U.S.

A more valuable contribution would be to note that public-sector activities do produce such external diseconomies as conges-tion, environmental pollution and international instability. This means that a positive theory of the state cannot rely solely on the theory of public goods for its foundation.

2 The Theory of Externalities and the Provision of Public Goods

Reverting to pure theory, let us recall some of the typical theorems of the firm and the household based on the pure independence assumption referred to in the opening paragraphs above.[1]

The private householder acting on his own will maximise utility by equating marginal rates of substitution to relative prices.[2] The individual firm will maximise profit by equating the marginal revenue product of a factor of production to its price (or by equating marginal revenue and marginal cost). More generally, any decision unit will decide the quantity of any activity (purchase or sale) by relating its marginal benefit to him to its marginal cost to him.

Let us now examine the pure public good. Although by definition others will benefit if he acquires it, a person may still buy some quantity of a good if the benefit that accrues to him exceeds the cost. In other words, it is perfectly possible for some of a public good to be provided privately. The condition is simply that it should be obtainable in a small enough quantity so that for at least one individual its benefits are greater than its costs.

[1] The assumption of pure independence may, in the case of households, be interpreted as one of selfishness. The term is rather less fitting for firms, but is not wholly inapposite there either. In making this assumption more frequently than another, economists might seem to be adopting the view that pure independence was the normal case and anything else rather a peculiar form of behaviour. In fact, the kind of empirical studies which might throw light on this issue have not been undertaken, and the normality of selfishness may be seen as a matter of analytical convenience within economic theory rather than anything else. It certainly seems to be the case that people recognise certain areas of activity as ones in which selfishness is not appropriate either for themselves or others.

[2] We ignore the cases where there is more than one constraint.

If the good is divisible and the normal maximisation conditions hold, for the ith person who purchases some of the good it will be true that the marginal rate of substitution between this and any other good will equal their relative prices (or its marginal utility will equal its price times the marginal utility of money), i.e.

$$\frac{U_{1j}}{U_{ij}} = \frac{P_1}{P_i} \qquad i = 2, \ldots, n$$

where good 1 is the public good, and person j buys some of it.

If person j buys a quantity of the public good X_{1j}, the total available to all people is $\sum_{j=1}^{J} X_{1j}$. (Since many people will not buy the public good at all, many of the X_{1j} will be zero.) The important thing is that what each person buys is available to all, which means that there is a sense in which the quantity of the good purchased and made available is not the same as the quantity consumed. This is in contrast to the private-good case where the quantity available to a person is the amount he purchases.

Let us now ask whether the total quantity of the public good so purchased is optimal in the sense of welfare maximisation. There are many different ways of showing that in general it is not. Consider an individual who purchases some of the public good, and for whom the tangency condition given above holds. A further small purchase of the public good is not worth while to him because its additional utility is less than the loss of utility resulting from a decrease in the quantity of some other good he must give up. The quantity of the good he has to give up is, of course, indicated by the ratio of its price to that of the public good, P_1/P_i. If, however, he had to give up a smaller quantity of the private good, he would be willing to purchase some more of the public good. Suppose now that at least one other person in the economy has a positive marginal utility from the public good. (There will clearly be such a person if the tangency condition holds for at least two people in the economy.) He could pay something for some additional quantity of the public good and be no worse off. If the second man did pay this, his welfare position would be unchanged, and our initial person's welfare would rise because he would be able to obtain an increment of the public good for its price less this payment. Because our initial person is capable of being made better off (as may other people) and nobody is made worse off, the initial position reached by independent maximisation is not Pareto optimal.

A much more direct way of getting to the same result is to note that for any individual the net benefit in money terms from an infinitesimal increase in the public good is equal to $\dfrac{U_{1j}}{U_{mj}}$ (where U_{mj} is the marginal utility of money), times the infinitesimal increase. The total net benefit to all of them is given by the sum of $\dfrac{U_{1j}}{U_{mj}}$ for all individuals. The cost to them is the price of the public good, P_1, multiplied by the infinitesimal increase. For at least one person, $\dfrac{U_{1j}}{U_{mj}}$ equals P_1; therefore, as long as U_{1j}/U_{mj} is positive for at least one other individual, total net benefit could be increased by this infinitesimal increase in the public good.

The increase in total net benefit minus total cost to the community is given by

$$\left(\sum_{j=1}^{J} \frac{U_{1j}}{U_{mj}} - P_1 \right) dX_1$$

where X_1 is the public good.

Since $\dfrac{U_{1j}}{U_{mj}}$ equals P_1 for one person, and is assumed positive for others, the expression in brackets is positive, and therefore an increase in total benefit could result from an increase in the quantity of the public good. Indeed, the above expression also leads to the condition for the quantity of the public good which maximises total welfare. It is that no further change in the quantity of the public good can add to total utility. This is possible only if the bracketed expression is zero, i.e.

$$\sum_{j=1}^{J} \frac{U_{1j}}{U_{mj}} = P_1.$$

In other words, the sum over all individuals of the marginal rates of substitution between the public good and money should equal its price. This contrasts with the maximisation condition for a private good which is that for each individual the marginal rate of substitution between his own quantity and money should equal its price. Those who do not trust the mathematics should see that the two conditions make good sense because in one case an extra unit of the good benefits all, and in the other case only its purchaser.[1]

It is possible to deal with some of these points using a simple diagram, as in Fig. 1 (Turvey [39]). Assume we are dealing with two people and one activity, and that the net benefit from the activity is expressible for each of them in interpersonally comparable money terms. (This benefit can be interpreted either as a measure of the gain in welfare for each of them resulting from the activity being operated at a particular level, or as the loss of welfare resulting from the activity not being operated at that level. When the marginal utility of income is constant, i.e. marginal effects of the activity are small relative to total welfare, these two interpretations are the same.)

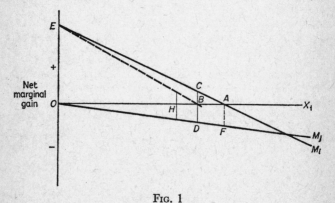

FIG. 1

The scale of the activity X_1 is measured on the horizontal axis. Net marginal gain, given by the curve M_i for person i and M_j for person j, is measured on the vertical axis. Net marginal gain may be positive or negative.

If the activity is controlled by i it will be operated in his own

[1] It should also be quite clear that the general principles hold, but the analysis is more complex where there are several public goods and where second-best constraints hold as well.

narrow interest at the level OA, where net marginal gain is zero. The total gain to him will be OEA. The marginal loss to j will be AF, and his total loss OAF. Taking the two of them together, their joint marginal loss will also be AF, indicating that by co-operation they can do better. (Note that this is compatible with the possibility that their total benefit, $OEA - OAF$, even at the suboptimal scale OA, is positive.)

If the activity is controlled by j it will be operated in his own narrow interest at a zero level. The marginal loss to j is zero, but the marginal benefit to i is OE, so that jointly they can gain by increasing the scale of the activity.

The optimal scale of the activity for the two of them together is where the marginal gain to one offsets the marginal loss to the other. In Fig. 1 this is the scale OB (i.e. $BC=BD$). Note that this optimal scale is determined by the marginal benefit curves M_i and M_j, and not by who decides the scale of the activity.

If person i controls the scale of the activity he will agree to its adjustment from OA to OB only if he does at least as well in the latter position as in the former. Since in the move he loses welfare to an extent measured by ABC, he will require at least that much compensation to make the move. But person j gains $BAFD$ (greater than ABC) by the reduction in scale, so he is able to compensate A and leave a net sum, $BAFD - ABC$, to be divided between them. This division of the net gain may be a matter of relative bargaining strengths, or subject to voluntary or compulsory arbitration, or other rules of society.

If person j controls the scale of the activity, he will need compensation at least equal to OBD to get him to move to the optimum point, but since person i gains $OBCE$ (greater than OBD), such compensation is feasible. Again there is a net surplus of $OBCE - OBD$ to be divided between them.

Note that the size of the surplus depends on who has the right to decide the scale of the activity, as does the benefit that each gains from it. But, as we have pointed out above, the optimum scale of provision is independent of that consideration.

Now, this diagram has been discussed in terms of two people, but it can be interpreted in terms of two classes of people, and can even be extended to encompass several classes of people. (Also, of course, other shapes of curves can be introduced to cover such cases as where they both gain or where there is more than one scale at which the sum of marginal benefits is zero, that is, there are several *local* optima, so called.) In that case the important point to remember is that, while the formal analysis still holds, real restrictions on co-operation and negotiation may prevent the optimum being reached, or the costs of achieving voluntary agreement may outweigh the benefits of reaching it. The practical choice may then be between one of two scales, zero and OA, corresponding to a ban or no control at all.

Another point to note concerns the taxation of the activity. Suppose the activity is controlled by person i, but is taxed so that his net benefit curve becomes the dotted line EB. It looks as if in that circumstance he will operate at the optimum scale OB, although his welfare will, of course, have been reduced. If, however, once the tax has been imposed, the proceeds are distributed to neither of them, i and j may co-operate again to maximise their joint welfare and choose the scale OH. If the purpose of the tax was simply to reach the scale OB it will thus have been defeated.

The final point to note concerns the existence of a second activity X_2, incompatible with X_1. It is possible that, acting alone, person i will choose to operate X_1 rather than X_2, but yet the joint optimum involves the use of X_2 and not X_1. This is illustrated in Fig. 2. Here, the curves are drawn so that the net

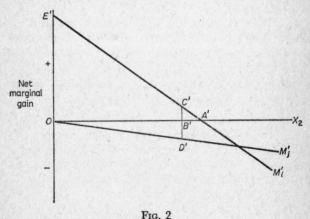

Fɪɢ. 2

marginal gain to the two of them, equal to $OE'C'B' - OB'D'$, is greater than the net marginal gain from X_1. Thus, if person i were allowed to operate the activity but obliged to compensate person j for all damages, he would choose activity X_2, and

28

operate it at the optimum level OD', while reducing the scale of X_1 to zero.

The analysis of taxation in this case is illustrated in Fig. 3.

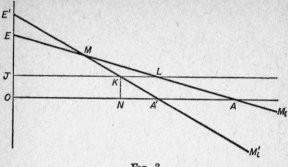

FIG. 3

At zero taxation, activity X_1 is operated at OA and X_2 at zero because the net gain OEA is greater than $OE'A'$. As we raise the tax per unit the advantage of X_1 falls relative to X_2, and at a rate of OJ per unit person i is indifferent between the two. At this point the net gain is the same, i.e. $EE'M = KLM$. At a still higher rate of tax, person i will operate X_2 and not X_1. It follows that, if the joint optimum scale of activity for X_1 is greater than ON (with X_2 equal to zero), or that of X_2 less than ON (with X_1 equal to zero), we can reach the optimum using a tax policy (subject to the constraint on further co-operation between i and j). But if the optimum were for X_1 to be operated between zero and ON, or for X_2 to be operated above ON, a tax policy would fail to bring it about.

The analysis of public goods and externality is correctly to be interpreted as a critique of private provision and part of the justification for public provision, although in no case is it decisive merely on its own. The question then arises as to the relative scale of public and private provision. Buchanan and Kafoglis [7] and Olson and Zeckhauser [29] have shown that this has a surprising aspect even in simple cases.

We shall consider their specific example, but the result is much more general than that. It concerns immunisation against a particular disease, and we make the somewhat unreal assumption that A's immunisation benefits him alone, but B's benefits him and A. Assume that the cost per shot of immunisation is constant and the same for each of them.

29

Let B choose a scale of immunisation that suits him alone, i.e. his marginal benefit equals the cost per unit. This is essentially a free gift to A, who will buy further shots up to the point at which his marginal benefit equals the cost per unit. The total amount of immunisation *purchased* is equal to what A buys plus what B buys. The total amount of immunisation *received* is that plus what B buys, i.e. what B buys is counted twice because each of them enjoys the benefit.

Consider the expansion of A's scale of immunisation. He is the only beneficiary and he has equated his marginal benefit to marginal cost; thus, the scale of his activity appears to be Pareto optimal. Consider B's scale of immunisation. An extra shot purchased by him will benefit both of them, but since he has not taken A's marginal benefit into account, he has chosen a scale of immunisation which is not Pareto optimal. The correct scale of immunisation for B is where his marginal benefit plus A's equal marginal cost.

Assume now that B's marginal benefit becomes zero at some level of immunisation so that all further benefits accrue to A no matter who is immunised. It would then be the case that the optimal scale of immunisation is where A's marginal benefit equals the cost per unit. Ignoring income effects, this is exactly the same scale as occurs in the non-Pareto situation. The difference is that more immunisation is provided by B (who also receives more benefit) and less by A. Total immunisation *purchased* is exactly the same in the collective as in the free market case, but the former is more efficient in that more immunisation is *received*.

This is illustrated in Fig. 4, where D_A measures the benefit to A and D_B that to B. C–C is the average and marginal cost curve. If A and B behave independently of each other, B will purchase OE shots and A, EF. Total shots purchased will be OF, and total immunisation received $OF + OE$.

The line S_B measures cost per unit less B's marginal benefit for quantities above OE. It is, as it were, B's supply curve of immunisation for A. For quantities beyond OG the supply curve reverts to C–C.

If A and B act jointly, B will purchase OG immunisation shots and A, GF. The total purchased will remain the same, but the total immunisation received will rise to $OF + OG$, a net increase of EG.

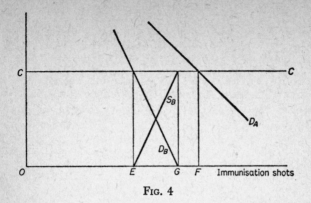

FIG. 4

If it is assumed that immunisation by B is a more than perfect substitute for A than his own immunisation, an increase in the number of shots by B would lead to a greater reduction in the number of shots to be provided by A. In that case the total quantity of immunisation *purchased* in the collective case would actually be less than in the free market case, although the immunisation received would be more. This makes good sense, because B has been assumed to be the efficient producer of immunisation, and optimum provision requires taking that into account.

It is worth noting that it was the originators of this aspect of the discussion who differentiated collective provision from free market provision in this way for this particular problem. Despite that, there seems no reason why in this case A and B should be unable to reach the optimum position voluntarily, although if each really designates many people, that is unlikely to happen.

The analysis so far pertains to pure public goods and to goods with a public-good content. It is also as well to make clear at this point what we have shown and what we have not shown. We have explained in a particular case that there exists a possible state of affairs superior to that arrived at by independent welfare maximisation. We have not explained whether arrangements can be made to reach that superior state or what those arrangements might be. We have not explained how the public good is to be provided and who is to pay for the extra amount. We have not considered whether policies to deal with public bads are the same in general as those for public goods except for

31

a reversal of direction, so to speak. We have assumed perfect divisibility of the goods, and we have ignored the phenomenon of altruism.

On the question of payment, let us start with the simplest possible example. Suppose there is a fixed indivisible quantity of the public good that may be provided. Suppose it is true that the total monetary benefit received by the individuals comprising the economy is greater than the price of the public good, and that it is not regarded as a public bad by any person. Assume also that the value of the benefit received by any one person is less than the price of the public good. In these circumstances the good will be provided only if the citizens can agree jointly to provide it. For the good to be provided privately people must be willing to contribute voluntarily, and they must be willing to reveal their true benefits from it, if contributions are to be related to these benefits.

Consider now the position of any individual. As long as his contribution is less than the value of the benefit he receives, he will gain from the provision of the public good. But, given this gross benefit, his net benefit will increase as his contribution decreases, i.e. as other people's contributions increase. This suggests that it will pay him to go to considerable lengths to avoid contributing to the finance of the public good, especially as, if it is provided by others, *ex definitione*, he cannot be prevented from enjoying its benefits. Thus, his best strategic approach to the provision of public goods is to play down his own likely benefit from the good, and to go to whatever lengths are likely to assist him in avoiding payment.[1]

The question then arises as to whether voluntary action is likely to occur. It is by no means certain that it is, but equally theory does not rule it out as impossible. As Arrow [1] has pointed out: 'It is a mistake to limit collective action to state action: many other departures from the anonymous atomism of the price system are observed regularly. Indeed, firms of any complexity are illustrations of collective action, the internal allocation of their resources being directed by authoritative and hierarchical controls.' If the relevant groups of beneficiaries are small, each can see more easily the advantages of joint action,

[1] We are discussing a situation known in game theory as the 'prisoner's dilemma' (Rapaport [32]). A book which discusses a great many of these problems in considerable detail is Olson [28].

and the disadvantages of independent behaviour and a failure to agree. The smallness of the group and the ease of communication might then be thought to lead them to the correct provision of the public good. Even here, however, it is not obvious that, if the selfishness assumption of orthodox economics holds, each individual will reveal his true benefit. Preferences may be revealed by private behaviour but not by public behaviour. This means that strategic behaviour could still lead to non-provision or at least generate difficulties about payment of contributions.

As the size of the group increases, so does difficulty of communication. In addition, the possibility of anonymity for any individual increases. This implies a rise in organisation costs, and many more problems in persuading people to contribute voluntarily.

This suggests the following conclusions:

(a) Voluntary organisation of the provision of a public good may depend on the size of the group receiving its benefits. Increased size may involve organisation costs to be set against benefits.

(b) Organisation of voluntary provision may depend on an if–then basis for contributions, i.e. a pledge to contribute if others contribute as well.

(c) Some rule must be introduced to deal with under-reporting of benefits, e.g. relating these to such simple objective criteria as income or age.

(d) The ability of a voluntary body to provide a public good may depend on its ability to supply a private good jointly with it. People will then join the organisation for the sake of the private benefits and in doing so be charged for a share of the public good too. It is sometimes suggested that bodies such as trade unions and the motoring organisations come under this heading (Olson [28]).

(e) In practice, voluntary provision may depend on altruism rather than on the selfishness assumption we have been making.[1]

---

[1] We are not, of course, arguing that voluntary behaviour does not occur or that it is irrational. On the contrary, it does exist and is important, but appears not to fit very well into mainstream economic reasoning.

The alternative to voluntary arrangements would be some public activity; people may recognise the existence of public goods and the problems that arise in determining their financing, and decide that a public sector could solve these problems on a compulsory basis. Note that the existence of public goods provides a basis for public provision. There are still plenty of problems remaining. Thus, without going too far into the principles of taxation, if tax contributions are to be related to benefits, there will remain for the public authorities the need to discover the true benefits received by people while it will still pay these people to disguise what they gain. (The total benefits will also have to be calculated in order to be compared with total costs to consider whether the public good is worth providing at all.) Since the public authorities will have to use fairly simple rules of taxation based on objectively observable criteria, there must inevitably be some departures from the benefit principle. In agreeing to public provision, therefore, an individual could still find himself a loser.[1]

Incidentally, public activity here might mean several different things. The good itself may be provided directly to the community by the public authorities. Alternatively, the public authorities might merely subsidise its price down to the level at which total individual purchase of the good would maximise the community's welfare. A further alternative would be for the public authorities to make purchase of the good compulsory and then devote its own energies to enforcement of its rules. Possibly, the 'purest of the pure' public goods would be of the first kind, but the other two alternatives exist as both theoretical and practical possibilities. Even in the defence field, state subsidies of rifles and ammunition come in the second category, and

---

[1] Thus, the public sector may behave somewhat arbitrarily and infringe the principle of Pareto optimality for administrative reasons. The emphasis here should, of course, be on 'arbitrarily', since it is hard to see how extreme Pareto optimality (i.e. nobody should ever be made worse off) can be applied in practice. Change is constantly taking place in the market economy leading to arbitrary variations in individual welfare, so that no fundamental new principle arises in connection with the operations of the public sector.

In considering whether the rule for a 'Pareto improvement' has been broken, the crucial problem is to decide in conditions of dynamic uncertainty what is a change and what is the *status quo*.

compulsory military service in the third. It may be partly a matter of political principle and partly a matter of organisational costs as to which method is selected.[1]

Some economists have endeavoured to use the theory of public goods as a theory for the formulation of the public sector, and to discuss such questions as: Under what circumstances would an individual agree to the setting up of a public sector?[2] What voting rules should a person agree to for public-sector decisions – simple majority, two-thirds, unanimity? And under what circumstances would an individual vote for one set of public authorities rather than another? As we have remarked, because of the difficulties of assessing individual benefits, a person is always in danger of losing from public-sector activity even if it is restricted to the pure public goods case. More to the point, public authorities may not be, and usually are not, restricted in such a way. As independent bodies, at least in the short term, they may have power to choose their own field of operation. What is more, we have shown that public activity is not necessarily implied by the existence of public goods. For all these reasons a positive theory of the existence and behaviour of the public sectors that are actually observed needs a broader and more solid foundation than the existence of pure public goods or even externalities. In particular, the public authorities

[1] In the case of public bads the relevant policies are taxes, rationing, and outright bans.

[2] Buchanan and Tullock [9]; Buchanan [6]. Much of the writing in this field lays special stress on Pareto optimality. It is as well to mention at this point the weakness of this criterion. If it is used to compare all possible activities (or 'states of the world'), it will not lead in general to one choice as superior to all others, but will instead give rise to a large number of alternatives each of which makes some people better off and some worse off than they would be in other situations. In other words, it will be impossible to choose between them simply according to the condition that nobody should lose and at least one person should gain. If the criterion is used in a more limited way to decide whether to move from the *status quo*, then apart from the problem of specifying the *status quo* there is the contradiction that the existing situation is justified according to a different criterion than all other situations. One vote is required to maintain the situation, unanimity (or unanimity, ignoring abstentions) to change it. In sum, the Pareto criterion is either incomplete or biased.

35

may exist for other reasons, but then turn to public goods as suitable fields for activity.

All that we have argued about the simple case of the fixed-quantity public good applies *a fortiori* to the situation in which the quantity can be varied. The decision problem is now much more complicated because of the need in assessing optimal scale to discover how individual benefits vary with scale. There may be many scales at which benefits exceed costs, and it is necessary to discover that one at which the difference is at a maximum. Further difficulties again arise from the use of tax rules only imperfectly related to individual benefits. As the scale of the public good varies, different people will find themselves arbitrarily paying more in taxes than they receive in benefits, and this excess of cost over benefits will itself not be constant.

More complications arise from the existence of other dimensions to the public good (or the existence of a band of many public goods, all of which are close substitutes). The quality of the public good may vary. While it remains a public good, it may still be possible to vary it in such a way as to benefit certain people more than others. It is clear, therefore, that the relevant decision problem is a far cry from the simple one of whether or not to provide the public good at all. This suggests three conclusions:

(*a*) A great deal of professional expertise is required in the field of public goods provision.

(*b*) The kind of financing procedures available to a voluntary organisation may not work at all.

(*c*) In many if not all cases, if the good is to be provided it is much more likely to emerge in the public sector. It is equally likely that administrative costs will be a significant part of the cost-benefit appraisal of public goods provision.

On the question of indivisibility, if the minimum quantity of the good that can be provided is very large relative to any individual household's or firm's command over resources, this may limit voluntary organisation, partly because no small voluntary group could be started up to gain some initial experience, and partly because the risk would be too large for the private sector to undertake.

At this point, let us look at the case of the public bad and see if that requires us to modify our analysis. It is easy to see that it does not. In the case of the public good, everyone benefits no matter who provides the good. If the good is sufficiently large and indivisible it will not be present at all unless its provision is organised jointly. If the public bad is not present there is, of course, no problem. The objective with respect to a public bad, therefore, is its removal or limitation. Indeed, the reduction of a public bad is exactly akin to the provision of a public good. This may be seen most easily by noting that the public good provided by defence is to remove the public bad generated by foreign military activity. It follows that few additional results ensue from the pure case of the public bad.

Incidentally, this leads to the obvious conclusion that, just as the optimum quantity of a public good will not be infinity, the optimum quantity of a public bad need not be zero. The costs of reducing the scale of the bad that is there must be offset against the benefits resulting therefrom.

There are, however, two further questions which are worth mentioning here. Many public goods or bads arise as joint products with purely private activities. (We are involved with the public good or bad content of those activities rather than with pure public goods or bads.) Air pollution from motor-cars and commercial vehicles is one example. Reduction in the spread of contagious disease from good personal hygiene is another. (It is sometimes suggested that public bads are much more likely than public goods to be jointly supplied with private goods.) In addition, there are many different ways of achieving desired public ends, and in the case of public bads one approach is to ban them or the activities which generate them. At the very least, such activities may be restricted in various ways. When it comes to public goods, while their provision may be encouraged by the public authorities, in practice in our society it may be very much harder to make them compulsory.[1] Thus, the treatment of public goods and bads may be asymmetric although they themselves are not.

[1] Compulsion is not impossible even in a free society. We do, for example, have a minimum school-leaving age partly on the grounds that staying at school is a public good. We also have compulsory third-party insurance in motoring, and compulsory seat belts in cars.

We have referred already to the selfishness assumption, which is that a person is concerned only with the goods and services which he buys or sells. While only his own goods and services enter into his utility or production function no difficulty arises with this concept. Once, however, public goods, or, more generally, externalities, exist, matters become a great deal more complicated. We have already said that in the case of the public good, if X_{1j} is the quantity purchased by the jth person, $X_1 = \sum_j X_{1j}$ is the quantity available to every person.

The variable X_1 will appear in everybody's utility function. We then argued that an individual would only buy a quantity X_{1j} up to the point where its marginal utility (i.e. of $\sum X_{1j}$) equalled its price, although at that point the marginal utility of this quantity to others would be positive. This is the basis of the suboptimality theorem as it appears in the literature.[1] Now, it might be thought that this could be dealt with if people were altruistic in the sense that they took account in their own utility functions of other people's welfare from the public good. The difficulty with this view is that the variable X_1 appears in each person's utility function, and that to take account of other people's utility of X_1 is still only to include X_1 in your own utility function. In other words, altruism defined in this way does not affect the formal description of the individual utility function.[2] To put the point differently, economists do not look behind the fact that an individual prefers more of X_1 to less. A person's preference for X_1 may derive from his concern for others or for himself, but the variable will appear in his utility function in the same way. It follows that the problem of public goods can remain in an other-regarding society. Difficulties also arise if the problem is approached in terms of behaviour and choice. At an elementary level, the problem of externality is discussed in terms of one person not taking into account the external benefits he provides or the external costs he imposes on

[1] A useful discussion is to be found in Bator [2]. He says, with respect to public goods (or 'public good externalities'): '. . . there are no decentralised organisational rearrangements, no private bookkeeping devices, which would, if only feasibility were not at issue, eliminate the difficulty' (p. 371).

[2] Obviously, a person who provides on his own a large enough quantity of X, such that its marginal utility to everybody else was zero, would have privately brought about the social optimum.

others. If we ask the question 'How do we know that this is so in any individual case?', it is apparent that, from the outside, so to speak, we do not know. It is quite possible that the factory producing the public bad of atmospheric pollution is taking the marginal disbenefit to others into account in deciding how much smoke to produce or how many smokeless boilers to introduce. Equally, a person building a fence may, in deciding its height, take his neighbour's interests into account. Note that the emphasis here is on possibility, not certainty, the point being an analytic and methodological one, namely, that it is never easy to determine the distortions due to externalities, rather than a substantive one that they do not exist or do not require group action.

To summarise so far, we have examined the pure public goods cases in terms of their relevance to group action and have seen that, while the two are obviously connected, there are a great many additional assumptions that have to be made before it can be assumed that group action is feasible or desirable, or that group action should be in the form of state action. Moreover, even when it is agreed that state action is feasible and desirable, this may take several forms. In addition, with respect to any public activity there remain choices concerning such matters as its desirable scale and desirable quality.

3 Externalities

When we go from the special case of pure public goods to the general case of externalities all these problems remain, and several more occur. In the remainder of this essay we shall concentrate on these new matters and not simply reiterate the old ones.

Let us start by examining an important contribution by Coase [11]. Assume one firm is engaging in an activity which represents an external diseconomy at the margin to another firm. If they behave independently of one another, they will arrive at a situation which is suboptimal for them and, in conditions of perfect competition, suboptimal for society. The correct scale of the external diseconomy-producing activity should be where its marginal addition to the two firms' profits taken together is zero. Now this state of affairs may be reached by the two firms getting together and deciding the level of the activity which the one firm regards as desirable and the other as undesirable. Alternatively, since joint action is more profitable than independent action, the externality may be 'internalised' and the firms may merge or one take over the other. This even provides us with the rudiments of a theory of the firm as such, i.e. what activities are determined by internal administration as opposed to the market. A firm may be defined as a means by which gains in efficiency are made by internalising external economies and diseconomies.[1] We may even take the argument further and note that if the external diseconomy is from a firm to a household, optimality may be reached by the latter purchasing the former and adjusting its policies appropriately.

In his article Coase is not concerned simply or mainly with

[1] There are also, of course, administrative costs and costs of using markets to be taken into account (see Coase [10]). Competitive conditions may actually force such mergers rather than merely indicate their desirability.

the fact that joint action is superior to independent action, but makes a much more important point in addition to that. In the case of the two firms there are two possibilities: one is that the offending firm has the right to engage in the activity; the other is that the harmed firm has the right to have the activity banned. Coase points out that the optimum scale of the offending activity does not depend on who has this right, although the distribution of income between the two firms and the relevant bargaining process may so depend.[1] In other words, we can say of this activity that one firm gains by increasing it from zero and the other loses, but we must also say that the first firm loses by reducing it from some level and the other gains. The theory of external economies and diseconomies is neutral between these two views and does not say where the relevant property right should be located. What it does make clear is the need for somebody, probably the state or the legal system, to determine where property rights lie. The state may also have a role to play where the interested parties cannot reach a successful agreement in the bargaining process. Where one or many firms pollute the atmosphere and cause many other firms and households to suffer, it is not apparent that the sufferers can move those causing the damage towards the optimum position without state action. Thus, while Coase's contribution is economically of great theoretical and philosophical significance, it still leaves a great area of potential public-sector activity.

Externalities give rise to some acute problems of income distribution. Concentrating again on external diseconomies, the effect of these, apart from the net welfare loss due to the misallocation of resources, is to make some people better off than they otherwise would be and others worse off. Although this may be viewed in a static context, more light is thrown on it in a dynamic one. If motor traffic develops along certain roads, its noise and other undesirable characteristics will be inflicted by some people and suffered by others. We have argued that if the former do not take these costs into account, it leads to a

[1] In the more general case, since the right is a form of property, there may be an income effect on the optimum position which modifies this conclusion slightly. His conclusion may also be modified to allow for bargaining and other costs of joint action, and the existence of market imperfections.

deadweight loss to the economy, some or all of which may be removable by public action. Apart from that, and even if it is corrected, there remains the loss to the people who suffer the external diseconomy. A similar point may be made about the siting of airports, factories, etc.

Now, it is possible to argue that the income distribution argument does not stand up. Firstly, some notion of swings and roundabouts could be put forward, suggesting that on average through his lifetime an individual gains at least as much by the external economies generated by the system as he loses by the external diseconomies and, while at any point of time he may complain about a particular external diseconomy, he is never willing to offer thanks for a whole series of external economies. Secondly, income distribution is correctly to be measured in terms of the discounted present value of lifetime streams of income by an age cohort. In arriving at such a figure all sorts of risks and uncertainties must be allowed for, and insurance can be bought for some of the risks. Included in these risks and uncertainties will be the externalities connected with membership of society, so that they will already have been taken into account. A similar point could then be made about any decision in that its potential externalities should, if it has been taken correctly, have been allowed for.

In reply to these arguments, it can immediately be said that there remain grounds for public corrective action to rectify mistakes. But this is not very helpful here, because such action could be justified to deal more generally with mistakes, and not with those resulting simply from externalities. More to the point surely is the view that, except in the most nebulous sense, many externalities simply cannot be predicted or meaningfully allowed for. If a man buys a house in the quiet countryside in a community of similar people and is then told that an airport is to be placed fairly close nearby, it is hard to see on what grounds he can be said to have taken this contingency into account (or ought to have), especially if he made this choice before aircraft had been invented. *A fortiori*, if the airport decision is itself being taken by a public authority, the issue may not simply be one of social cost and social benefit, but of which section of the community will pay the cost and which receive the benefit depending on where the airport is located. It is not easy in a democratic society for the public authority to argue that all such income distribution considerations can and must be left out of account because they have already been discounted simply as part of membership of the community. The sufferers can reply that this is not a random event, but a decision which has yet to be taken, and that on rational grounds some weight must be given to them as bearers of the cost.

There are, however, further points to be made. The first is to note that the argument in favour of ignoring income distribution does cause us to realise that the system adjusts for this to some extent and that it is possible to exaggerate the significance of income distribution effects. Thus, the existing owners of homes near airports may have purchased them subsequent to the development of the airport, in which case there is no loss of income to be attributed to them, but only to their predecessors whom it may be impossible to find. Similarly, people who choose to live in towns know that they are places where noise, dirt and congestion occur. (One cannot, of course, make such a facile point about those who are born in towns, but it is not obvious what birth can be regarded as committing one to, anyway!)

Secondly, it could be argued that income distribution as part of social welfare represents a special sort of externality. The reason why we worry about the generalised distributions between rich and poor is that this enters into our individual utility functions. We are concerned with the prevention of extreme poverty for the same reason. There is, of course, also the point that, if the poor lose utility because of the rich, while this may be an externality, it need not infringe Pareto optimality. The reason is that if the rich do not have the analogous externality (i.e. they lose utility because of the poor), the poor can only be made better off at the expense of the rich. It hardly seems likely, therefore, that poverty (and race, for that matter) can be dealt with satisfactorily chiefly in terms of externality.

A third point on income effects relates to the distinction between marginal and intra-marginal externalities (Buchanan and Stubblebine [8]). Suppose an activity causes a person a great deal of harm if it is performed at all, but that this harm does not vary with the scale of the activity. The marginal disbenefit is zero, but independent behaviour is not optimal if the total gain to the offending party is small. Thus, total utility conditions must be examined as well as marginal utility.[1] It could be the case, however, that the total gain to the offending party is larger than the harm to the sufferer, in which case independent behaviour is optimal, but might still be judged to be unfair to the person who is adversely affected.[2]

Reverting to the main theme, it is apparent that the activity giving rise to an externality will be at the wrong level, so to speak, if no action is taken to adjust for the externality. This does not mean that it is obvious what is the correct level for it, or even that it is always clear-cut whether it should be increased or decreased. Thus, an activity generating an external economy may necessarily go hand in hand with one generating an external diseconomy. It will then be necessary to weigh one against the other in determining the optimum adjustments.[3]

Following on from this, the same activity may be seen as beneficial by some and harmful by others. An obvious example is a crowded and noisy beach where some people's utility rises with the density of the crowd and the noise while others' falls. There is no obvious assignment of property rights to be agreed here, nor is there necessarily an allocative loss in that the sum of the external benefits might just equal the sum of the external costs, leaving the independently arrived-at result an efficient one.[4]

Concerning policy, there are two mistakes that need to be avoided. Firstly, while the fact that an activity generates an external diseconomy may imply that its level should be reduced,

[1] Second-order conditions must also be taken seriously into account (Baumol [3]).

[2] More generally, where there are indivisibilities, 'marginal' conditions must be adjusted to deal with the minimum size of unit in which the commodity is available or the minimum scale at which an activity can be undertaken.

[3] The field of transport offers copious examples: easier communication, national and international, may be socially beneficial but it involves noise, dirt and congestion. It is worth noting the extent to which externalities are interrelated and occur together. This is clearly so when they are due to such causes as population growth and income growth (see Mishan [24]).

[4] In cases like this fairness may require some beaches to be crowded and some not. The important point to realise is that it is a mistake to jump to conclusions as to whether a particular phenomenon is an external economy, or a diseconomy, or both.

this does not mean that it should be reduced to zero, but simply to the level where its marginal benefit equals the sum of its marginal private and social costs. This means that external economy-producing activities may be observed even in the optimum situation. It also means that the fact that a public enterprise in particular is seen to engage in such activities does not mean that it is behaving in a socially inefficient way. Of course, in practice sufficient information may not be available to adjust matters exactly, and external diseconomies, for example, may have to be dealt with by bans (Turvey [39]).

Coase is right to point out that the public sector may generate external diseconomies. Pylons that spoil the countryside are put there by the C.E.G.B.; aircraft noise comes from B.O.A.C. and B.E.A. flying to and from airports run by the B.A.A., the Board of Trade, and various municipalities. Public-sector vehicles are just as capable of occupying scarce road space as private-sector ones. What he cannot assume is that these bodies ignore the social effects of their actions as their private counterparts may well do (Coase [11]).

Apart from that, it is worth noting that the existence of a multiplicity of public authorities may itself give rise to externalities. External economies or diseconomies may spill over from one authority to another. (More correctly, the citizens of one authority will receive benefits or incur costs resulting from the activities of another authority. There is also the complication that the same person may belong for one purpose or another to several authorities.) Thus the costs of education may be borne by one part of the county (or one county) and the external benefits received by another part (or another county). Poor sewage disposal by one seaside resort may foul the beaches of neighbouring resorts. The removal of traffic congestion in one London borough may lead to its emergence in another. There is again no limit to possible examples. Equally, improved allocation of resources may result from voluntary co-operation or by the introduction of higher-level authorities. Both occur in the U.K. It may also be predicted that authorities will wish to act in their own interest similarly to individuals, namely, to emphasise costs and minimise benefits. There may be further difficulties in the way of voluntary co-operation derived from limitations on the taxing and borrowing power of authorities. A benefiting authority, for example, may not be able to transfer funds to another authority which incurs costs on behalf of its citizens. In general, if voluntary co-operation is possible and benefiting authorities can pay for what they receive, the effect will be to raise all participating authorities' welfare. Thus, if the spillover is an external economy, and is not an inferior good, more of it will be consumed in the co-operative situation than in the initial situation (Musgrave [26]; Williams [40]).

Secondly, it is important to direct policy towards the offending activity rather than a related one. In the production of a great many commodities it may be a particular factor input that causes the trouble. It is sometimes suggested that the way to deal with this is to tax the output so that less of it is sold. If, however, the offending input is an inferior factor, more of it will be used when output is reduced, thus accentuating social costs.[1] If the factor creates external diseconomies no matter how it is used, the correct tax will be on the factor itself. If, however, the externality depends on the factor being used in a particular process, the tax must be on the process. It is also important to note that the long-run adjustment to the tax may differ from the short-run, but the inferior factor phenomenon can arise in either case.

[1] Plott [31]. This useful article makes an original point and has not received the recognition it deserves. See also Fraser [14]. An excellent critical discussion of tax–subsidy policy for externalities is Ng [27].

4 Externalities and the Private Sector

The final main section of this essay is concerned with various aspects of the private-sector response to public goods and externalities of various kinds.

The fact that an activity is being carried on by the private sector does not mean, of course, that it has no public-sector ramifications or that it may not be better run in the public sector. We have remarked already that once an activity takes place at all, the cost of serving additional customers may be low or even zero. It may, however, still be possible to deal with customers on an individual basis (i.e. non-payers may be excluded) and charge them individually, possibly at some additional cost. One example would be a theatre working at less than capacity. Another would be radio or television transmissions that required special decoding devices. A third would be toll-gates on limited-access but uncongested roads or bridges.[1] (A pop festival in a large open space would come into this category if the organisers controlled the only means of access.)

What we have in these cases is a form of increasing returns or diminishing marginal cost along the dimension of number of people served.[2] A private-sector firm with monopoly power (i.e. confronted with a downward-sloping demand curve) could maximise profits and more than cover its costs, including the costs of charging and providing the service on an individual basis.

[1] This is to be distinguished from the case of congested roads where users place a cost on each other and where optimality requires a form of road pricing.

[2] It is important to distinguish this from the usual sense of decreasing marginal cost of the quantity of a commodity. A commodity may be produced in conditions of increasing marginal cost relative to its physical quantity and yet show diminishing or zero marginal cost relative to the number of people who can benefit from it.

The alternative would be to provide the service at marginal cost to the customer, which might well be zero. In this case total social benefit would rise by the benefits received by extra customers together with the savings resulting from neither having to administer a charging system nor from individualising the service. To be set against this would be extra costs resulting from financing the service in some other way (e.g. taxes), and lack of the kind of knowledge of demand revealed by a pricing system.

An interesting case would be that of an enterprise for which the price that people were willing to pay for a service would be sufficient to cover all costs except the charging process itself, but where the latter is sufficiently high so that at no price can total cost be covered. We then have the seeming paradox that the net benefits outweigh the cost, but any attempt to charge will lead to losses, as will free provision (Millward [23]).

Apart from that, there are the usual problems that raising tax revenues may themselves involve welfare losses and that there may be a redistribution of income from taxpayers in general to the users of the service. While it may be possible to invent rather complicated, discriminatory tax schemes, these have little or no relevance in practice. Again, therefore, the practical choice is between imperfect alternatives rather than the optima of pure theory.

Yet another approach, especially where marginal cost is still positive, but below price, would be to subsidise the service received per customer or, where they can be identified, to subsidise the customers who cannot afford the market price. To offset against this would be the costs of financing the subsidy, and possibly the desirability of taxing away in whole or part the extra profit accruing to the private enterprise.[1]

There is an additional kind of example where seemingly successful private response to public-sector activities is not optimal. It is a sort of counterpart to the case we have just discussed. The noise produced by an aircraft may be offset, possibly quite successfully, by insulating private houses within its range. Similarly, the pollution produced by factory effluent may be offset by water-purifying devices installed in private houses. In either case it might be argued that each household's

[1] This might require discriminatory profits taxes which might not be administratively feasible.

54

demand is at a price which at the margin measures its benefit so that total welfare is maximised, leaving only the question of distribution of income between households and those who generate external diseconomies.

It could be, however, that alternative methods exist to deal with these externalities but that these have the characteristics of public goods in that everybody benefits from their introduction and cannot be charged for that benefit. This would be so if it were possible to stop aircraft noise by modifying or changing the engine, or if the factory adopted cleaner processes or purified its effluent itself. Now it could be that the cost of these alternative methods is less that the total cost of all the individual devices bought by households. If this were so, a public-sector decision to place in the first instance the burden of dealing with the external diseconomy at its source would raise total welfare. The government might do this by giving households the right to sue firms who would then be obliged to calculate whether it would be more profitable to act directly on their own processes or on the houses themselves. Alternatively, it might subsidise the welfare-maximising process in firms while adjusting taxes to take account of income distribution effects. A third possibility would be to nationalise the firm and introduce the public-good process itself.

Finally, there is one extension of this case that is worth noting. It concerns the returns to research and development. Research and development in processes which have a public-good characteristic will not be profitable to the private sector and without an appropriate degree of altruism will not be carried out by it. At the same time, research and development in processes which households can buy individually may well be profitable. It could be of value to the community, therefore, if the public sector were to subsidise the former or, of course, carry it out itself.

5 Conclusion

The purpose of this essay has been to examine the concept of public goods in particular and external economies in general. These concepts have been thought by some economists to provide a positive explanation of the sort of activities actually undertaken in the public sector, and by others a normative explanation of the sort of activities which ought to be undertaken in the public sector. It is hoped that, while the relevance of public goods to these matters has been made clear, it is also apparent that we are a long way yet from a satisfactory theory of the public sector. There is a strong connection between public goods and public-sector activity, and it may be expected that what may eventually turn out to be a successful theory of the public sector will give a major role to public goods. But we are not there yet.

Apart from that, it must be emphasised that the great expansion of research and published work in this field in the past decade has been typical of economics in that, while being analytically powerful, imaginative, subtle and concerned with a vast range of possible cases, it has also strayed further and further from reality. The economist's great strength of showing that things are not what they seem, and that policy-making involves many pitfalls, is seen here to its best advantage. Equally, this is a field in which practical contributions are required, both by way of developing new methods and of applying them to pressing problems. Perhaps the next decade will see much more applied work on externalities and public goods.

Finally, great caution should be exercised in interpreting the results which we have arrived at. A great many arguments can be put forward as to why a decentralised privately operated economic system will lead to results which are socially unsatisfactory. Public goods and external effects are among these reasons, but there are others, such as inequalities of income, rejections of certain private preferences, and doubts about the processes of preference formation, which, while they might be squeezed into such categories, are best discussed in other terms.[1] Equally, it could be argued that ultimately all activities involve externalities in that they may affect society, or at least any individual may choose to poke his nose into them.[2] In a sense, therefore, all goods are public goods, which suggests that a great deal more is required by way of theory and value judgements to explain the behaviour of the state or to evaluate it.

[1] Margolis [19]. This major article has had little follow-up, although it raises questions of the utmost importance, as the following quotations indicate: 'Why are some forms of public services compulsory, free or rationed? The answers to these questions are vital to a theory of public expenditures, and unfortunately they require penetration into the murky waters of political sociology. . . . To explain the existence of public activities and to evaluate the efficiency of an allocation of the public budget we must refer to the structure of social values.'

[2] The *locus classicus* of this point is, of course, Robbins [33]: 'There is scarcely anything which I can do outside the privacy of my home which has not some of the overtone of indiscriminate benefit or detriment. The clothes I wear, the shows I frequent, the flowers that I plant in my garden, all directly, or through the mysterious influence of fashion, influence the enjoyment and satisfactions of others. Even what is done remote from the perception of others can be conceived to have this aspect. The fact that other people lead a way of life different from my own, that they like and buy pictures and books of which I disapprove and give private banquets of sacred meat and forbidden wines, can clearly be the occasion to me of the most intense mortification. Is this to be included in the calculus of external economies and diseconomies? I can think of few forms of totalitarian regimentation of consumption which could not find some formal justification by appeal to this analysis' (pp. 20–1).

Select Bibliography

[1] K. Arrow, 'Political and Economic Evaluation of Social Effects and Externalities', in J. Margolis (ed.), *The Analysis of Public Output* (Columbia U.P., New York, for N.B.E.R., 1970).

[2] F. M. Bator, 'The Anatomy of Market Failure', *Quarterly Journal of Economics* (1958).

[3] W. J. Baumol, 'External Economies and Second Order Optimality Conditions', *American Economic Review* (1964).

[4] W. J. Baumol, *Welfare Economics and the Theory of the State*, 2nd ed. (Bell, London, 1965).

[5] P. Bohm, 'Pollution, Purification and the Theory of External Effects', *Swedish Journal of Economics* (1970).

[6] J. M. Buchanan, *The Demand and Supply of Public Goods* (Rand McNally, Chicago, 1968).

[7] J. M. Buchanan and M. Kafoglis, 'A Note on Public Goods Supply', *American Economic Review* (1963).

[8] J. M. Buchanan and W. C. Stubblebine, 'Externality', *Economica* (1962).

[9] J. M. Buchanan and G. Tullock, *The Calculus of Consent* (Michigan U.P., Ann Arbor, 1962).

[10] R. H. Coase, 'The Nature of the Firm', *Economica* (1937).

[11] R. H. Coase, 'The Problem of Social Cost', *Journal of Law and Economics* (1960).

[12] R. Dorfman, 'General Equilibrium with Public Goods', in Margolis and Guitton [20].

[13] A. Downs, *An Economic Theory of Democracy* (Harper & Row, New York, 1957).

[14] R. D. Fraser, 'Externalities and Corrective Taxes: A Comment', *Canadian Journal of Economics* (1968).

[15] M. Friedman, *Capitalism and Freedom* (Chicago U.P., 1962).

[16] J. de V. Graaf, *Theoretical Welfare Economics* (Cambridge U.P., 1957).

[17] J. G. Head, 'Public Goods and Public Policy', *Public Finance* (1962).

[18] R. W. Houghton (ed.), *Public Finance* (Penguin Books, Harmondsworth, 1970).

[19] J. Margolis, 'A Comment on the Pure Theory of Public Expenditure', *Review of Economics and Statistics* (1954).

[20] J. Margolis and H. Guitton (eds), *Public Economics* (Macmillan, London, 1969).

[21] J. E. Meade, 'External Economies and Diseconomies in a Competitive Situation', *Economic Journal* (1952).

[22] J. E. Meade, *Trade and Welfare* (Oxford U.P., 1955).

[23] R. Millward, 'Exclusion Costs, External Economies and Market Failure', *Oxford Economic Papers* (1970).

[24] E. J. Mishan, *The Costs of Economic Growth* (Staples Press, London, 1967).

[25] E. J. Mishan, 'The Postwar Literature on Externalities: An Interpretative Essay', *Journal of Economic Literature* (1971).

[26] R. Musgrave, 'Provision for Public Goods', in Margolis and Guitton [20].

[27] Y. Ng, 'Recent Developments in the Theory of Externality and the Pigovian Solution', *Economic Record* (1971).

[28] M. Olson, *The Logic of Collective Action* (Harvard U.P., Cambridge, Mass., 1965).

[29] M. Olson and R. Zeckhauser, 'Collective Goods, Comparative Advantage and Alliance Efficiency', in R. N. McKean (ed.), *Issues in Defence Economics* (Columbia U.P., 1967).

[30] A. C. Pigou, *Economics of Welfare* (Macmillan, London, 1920).

[31] C. R. Plott, 'Externalities and Corrective Taxes', *Economica* (1966).

[32] A. Rapaport, *Fights, Games and Debates* (Michigan U.P., Ann Arbor, 1960).

[33] L. C. Robbins, *The Economic Problem in Peace and War* (Macmillan, London, 1947).

[34] P. A. Samuelson, 'The Pure Theory of Public Expenditure', *Review of Economics and Statistics* (1954).

[35] P. A. Samuelson, 'Diagrammatic Exposition of a Theory of Public Expenditure', *Review of Economics and Statistics* (1955).

[36] P. A. Samuelson, 'Aspects of Public Expenditure Theories', *Review of Economics and Statistics* (1958).

[37] P. A. Samuelson, 'Pure Theory of Public Expenditure and Taxation', in Margolis and Guitton [20].

[38] T. Scitovsky, 'Two Concepts of External Economies', *Journal of Political Economy* (1954).

[39] R. Turvey, 'On Divergencies between Social Cost and Private Cost', *Economica* (1963).

[40] A. Williams, 'The Optimal Provision of Public Goods in a System of Local Government', *Journal of Political Economy* (1966).